Launch Out Into the Deep

Launch Out Into the Deep

Keidra H. Hobley, PhD

Xulon Press

Xulon Press
2301 Lucien Way #415
Maitland, FL 32751
407.339.4217
www.xulonpress.com

© 2018 by Keidra H. Hobley, PhD

All rights reserved solely by the author. The author guarantees all contents are original and do not infringe upon the legal rights of any other person or work. No part of this book may be reproduced in any form without the permission of the author. The views expressed in this book are not necessarily those of the publisher.

Scripture quotations taken from the New King James Version (NKJV). Copyright © 1979, 1980, 1982, 1984 by Thomas Nelson, Inc. Used by permission. All rights reserved.

Scripture quotations taken from the Holy Bible, New Living Translation (NLT). Copyright ©1996, 2004, 2007, 2013 by Tyndale House Foundation. Used by permission of Tyndale House Publishers, Inc.

Printed in the United States of America.

www.keidrahobley.com

ISBN-13: 9781545627297

To my baby girl, Brielle. It was your carpool line that I was sitting in when God taught me this lesson and it was you, at the tender age of seven, who sat through each of my classes when I first taught this to others. You are wise beyond your years and an inspiration to us all.

CONTENTS

Introduction xi

Week 1: Launch Out Into the Deep? 1

Week 2: Wash Your Nets 7

Week 3: Let Jesus in Your Vessel 13

Week 4: Here Are Your Instructions 19

Week 5: This is Hard Work 25

Week 6: The Blessing of Help and Obedience 35

Week 7: The Beauty of Repentance and Humility 43

Week 8: Fishermen will be Fishermen 49

Week 9: This Way to the Deep 55

Week 10: Exactly What is Deep 61

Week 11: Preparing for the Deep 69

Week 12: Launching Out Into the Deep! 77

Introduction

I can remember it like it was yesterday. My family and I went to Cracker Barrel for lunch one Sunday afternoon after church. There was a significant wait time so my children took off to the toy section of the gift shop and I headed toward the household items. It was during the fall and all the Thanksgiving dishes were on display. As I was standing there looking at a Thanksgiving platter, I could feel a presence close behind me on my left side. Trying to be discreet, I didn't turn around. Instead, I just kept looking at the platter in front of me. Then, I felt "the presence" get a little closer. This time I decided I would turn around slightly so "the presence" would know I was aware she was there. I didn't want to make any sudden movements or come across as rude by just walking away, so I patiently lingered. About a minute later, she finally spoke up and said, "You like that, don't you?" Thinking that was kind of a weird question to ask, I turned slightly and responded, "It's Okay" and subtly took one step away. After a few more seconds she said, "Yeah, that would just collect dust in my house. But you… You would use it." "Okay" I thought to myself as I discretely took another, slightly bigger step away. "You're good at that kind of stuff," she stated quite matter-of-factly. Before I knew it I rattled out, "How do you know?" Her response to me was one I never expected. "Because I'm a prophet." "Oh, boy!" I thought to myself. "Here we go!" I don't know if it was just my suspicious nature or the fact that I was hungry and ready to eat, but the very next thought that went through my mind was, "Is she about to be prophesying or prophelying?"

Unmoved by whatever expression I may have had on my face at the time, she proceeded to share what she felt like she needed to say. As she talked, I thought to myself, "Yeah, yeah, yeah. That could apply to anybody." She continued and what she shared began to get a little more specific. Then I started to think, "Okay. I'm listening." The more she talked, the closer to home her words began to hit. I finally surrendered and said to myself, "Okay. Now you have my attention." As I intently listened, trying to hold on to every word, I knew God was using her to speak to me. She went on for several minutes. When she had said all she needed to say, she just stopped. Once she did, I quickly turned my head to check on my children and when I turned back around she was gone. I stood in one place and looked around but she was nowhere to be found. Had I just experienced an angel encounter or just a really fast old lady? I'm not really sure. But what I do know is I immediately went to my car, whipped out my pen and notebook as quickly as I could and wrote down everything I could remember her saying. The one statement that stood out to me above everything else she said was, "It's time for you to launch out into the deep."

INTRODUCTION

Launch out into the deep. Whoa! That one statement seemed to resonate with me and I didn't even know why. Later that evening, I called my older sister who lived in another state at the time and shared with her what happened. I had never experienced anyone speaking over me like that. We were both in awe. It was an experience that was forever imprinted in both of our long term memories.

Several months later, I was sitting in the carpool line waiting to pick my children up from school. While I was sitting there, I decided to check my voicemail. On my voicemail was an enthusiastic message from my older sister. She was telling me all about how someone came up to her at church the previous night and told her she needed to launch out into the deep! She could barely contain herself. The last thing she said in her message was, "I need you to tell me exactly what that means." I hung up from the voicemail and began to ponder, "Exactly what does that mean? I know there's a scripture in the Bible some where that says something about launch out into the deep but I don't know the reference and I'm not fully sure of the context." As I was about to press the call back button on my cell phone, I looked at the clock. I still had about 20 more minutes before the children's school bell was to ring so I thought to myself, "At least I can look up the scripture reference so I can let her know where to find it in the Bible."

Well, once I found the scripture and began to read it, it was like a river of supernatural revelation began to flow. It literally seemed like as I read each verse God was showing me what I needed to take from it and how I needed to apply it to my life. It was coming so fast I could barely keep up. I ended up just calling her back so I could share the revelation with her as it came. The phone rang and rang. As I sat there about to burst wide open, her voicemail picked up. At the sound of the beep, I took off like a jet plane and was spewing out revelation to the voicemail recorder like it was an audience of ten thousand! Six voicemail messages later, I had preached to her the whole scripture passage of Luke 5:1–11.

Once I got it all out over the voicemail, I then grabbed my pencil and attempted to document in my Bible next to each scripture what God had just revealed to me. The more I wrote, the more He showed me. The more He showed me, the more I wrote! Then, the school bell rang. Just like that, the Father had opened up the scriptures to me. After studying it out further, I shared it with a women's group at my church over the course of several weeks. After multiple requests to share it over and over again and after years later still hearing about the impact this teaching has had on people's lives, I completely understood when the Father told me this was the next book I was to write. This book is my way of sharing with the world what the Father shared with me. If you attempt to read it like a novel, you will gain some great information. But even better than that, if you

INTRODUCTION

take your time and work your way through it, I believe God will show you great revelation specific to your life.

I have written this book as a twelve week study to help you take bite-sized pieces and chew on them thoroughly. At the end of each chapter are questions that will help you fully digest what you have chewed on and make it much easier to apply what God has shown you to your everyday life. This book can be thoroughly enjoyed as an individual study or taken to an even greater level as a small group study. It is my prayer that it blesses you as much as it blessed me that day many years ago while sitting in the carpool line.

Week 1

Launch Out Into the Deep?

What comes to mind when you hear the term *launch out into the deep*? Well, as I began to study this out, I did what any good student would do. I pulled out my Merriam Webster Dictionary and defined each word in the term. *Launch* is a verb that means to release, to catapult, a self-propelled object, to set in motion, to get off to a good start, to enter energetically or to blast off. The definition I like the most out of these is *a self-propelled object*. *Out* means in a direction away from among others, away from the shore, away from home or work, away from a particular place, into the possession or control of another (as in to lend out money), to completion or satisfaction (as in hear me out or work the problem out), to the full or a great extent or degree (as in all decked out or stretched out) and in or into the open (as in the sun came out). The first one, *in a direction away from among others*, is the definition I like for this one. *Into* means entry, introduction, insertion, involved with, interested in, in the direction of or toward a position of contact. *Toward a position of contact* seems to define this one well.

At this point you may be wondering, "Did she really look up the word *the*?" Yes, she sure did and it actually had a definition. According to the dictionary, the word *the* is used as a function word to indicate that a following noun or noun equivalent is definite or has been previously specified by context or by circumstance. Here, let's focus on the phrase *definite or has been previously specified*. Of all the words, *deep* probably had the most definitions to choose from. It means extending far beyond the surface or the superficial, extending well inward, near the outer limits of the playing area, a place too far to be seen with the natural eye, difficult to penetrate or comprehend, mysterious, unknown, unseen, obscure, intensely engrossed or immersed or being below the level of consciousness. Would you like to guess which of these definitions stood out to me the most? *Difficult to penetrate or comprehend.*

So, the way my brain works, I thought if I'd take all the definitions of the individual words and put them together, I would have the definition of the term. So, that's exactly what I did. The definition of the term *launch out into the deep* that I came up with was one that was intensely profound and completely unexpected:

Launch Out Into the Deep:
To propel yourself in a direction away from among others toward a position of contact that is definite or has been previously specified but that you may find difficult to penetrate or comprehend.

LAUNCH OUT INTO THE DEEP?

Pretty good, huh? I thought so! To propel yourself – you're going to have to do some work. In a direction away from among others – you're going to have to sanctify yourself. Toward a position of contact that is definite or has been previously specified – God has a plan for your life. That you may find difficult to penetrate or comprehend – God never said fulfilling the plan He has for your life would be easy or that you would always understand why He's instructing you to do certain things a certain way, but He expects you to obey anyway.

So, where does this term come from? It comes from Luke 5:4 which says, "When He had stopped speaking, He said to Simon, "Launch out into the deep and let down your nets for a catch." The *He* that is referred to here is Jesus. So, let's read it this way, "When [Jesus] had stopped speaking, He said to Simon, "Launch out into the deep and let down your nets for a catch." Now, to really bring this all to life, let's read the verse in context.

> So it was, as the multitude pressed about Him to hear the word of God, that He stood by the Lake of Gennesaret, and saw two boats standing by the lake; but the fishermen had gone from them and were washing their nets. Then He got into one of the boats, which was Simon's, and asked him to put out a little from the land. And He sat down and taught the multitudes from the boat. When He had stopped speaking, He said to

Simon, "Launch out into the deep and let down your nets for a catch." But Simon answered and said to Him, "Master, we have toiled all night and caught nothing; nevertheless at Your word I will let down the net." And when they had done this, they caught a great number of fish, and their net was breaking. So they signaled to their partners in the other boat to come and help them. And they came and filled both the boats, so that they began to sink. When Simon Peter saw it, he fell down at Jesus' knees, saying, "Depart from me, for I am a sinful man, O Lord!" For he and all who were with him were astonished at the catch of fish which they had taken; and so also were James and John, the sons of Zebedee, who were partners with Simon. And Jesus said to Simon, "Do not be afraid. From now on you will catch men." So when they had brought their boats to land, they forsook all and followed Him. (Luke 5:1–11)

❧ Applying the Word ☙

I chose to do this study because…

_____
_____
_____
_____
_____
_____
_____

What I hope to get out of this study is…

_____
_____
_____
_____
_____
_____
_____

To me, the term *launch out into the deep* means…

_____
_____
_____
_____
_____
_____

As a result of reading this passage of scripture, God has already begun speaking to me about…

_____
_____
_____
_____
_____
_____
_____

I'm going to start applying this to my life by…

_____
_____
_____
_____
_____
_____
_____

But don't just listen to God's word. You must do what it says.
Otherwise, you are only fooling yourselves.
James 1:22 NLT

Week 2

Wash Your Nets

Now, that we have established a foundation for the term *launch out into the deep*, let's begin to look at Luke 5:1–11 verse by verse. Verses 1–2 say:

> So it was, as the multitude pressed about Him to hear the word of God, that He stood by the Lake of Gennesaret, and saw two boats standing by the lake; but the fishermen had gone from them and were washing their nets.

Notice the word *multitude* and notice the word *hear*. If the multitudes were able to hear Jesus, then Jesus either had to be talking extremely loud or His voice was being projected in some way. The Bible says in Romans 10:17 that faith comes by hearing, and hearing by the Word of God. So, if the multitudes were hearing, then their faith was being built. Anyone anywhere near that area had to have heard Jesus and their faith was being built also. I would think that would include the fishermen who were washing their nets nearby.

The verse says Jesus stood by the Lake of Gennesaret. If you were to look at a map, you would notice the Lake of Gennesaret is right along the edge of a major body of water – the Sea of Galilee. Do you know what other miraculous things happened on this body of water? We're told in Matthew 14:22-33 that Jesus walked on it! So, just from that alone, we should already expect supernatural things to happen here!

As Jesus stood by the Lake of Gennesaret, what did He see? He saw two boats. What kind of boats were these? Do you think they were two blow-up rafts? Two row boats? How about two canoes? Maybe we can better answer this question if we ask ourselves who these two boats belonged to. Did they belong to people who fished just for fun? No. These boats belonged to men who fished for a living. So, these boats had to be some sort of commercial fishing vessels if they were owned by professional fishermen.

At the end of verse two, we find these fishermen washing their nets. To me, this suggests the fishermen weren't doing anything out of the ordinary. They were not engaging in some super spiritual activity. They were simply going about their normal routine. I'm not a fisherman, so I had to do a little research on fishing nets. When I did, I learned that nets can become brittle, rough and unusable if they're not washed frequently. If they're used after becoming hardened, they can cause damage to whatever they catch. I also learned that nets can spread disease to other healthy fish if they're not continuously washed.

WASH YOUR NETS

The Bible tells us in Ephesians 5:26 that we have to be washed in the water of the Word. So, just like natural fishing nets, we can become brittle, rough, and unusable if we're not washed in the Word frequently. Then, if we're not careful, if we attempt to minister to other people after becoming hardened we can cause damage to whomever we "catch." Also like nets, we can spread dis-ease to other healthy people if we're not continuously being washed in the water of the Word.

Now, let's go back to the fisherman. The simple fact that they were washing their nets suggests to me that even though they hadn't caught anything that night, they had not made the emotional decision to completely give up on fishing altogether. They weren't throwing their nets away. They were preparing them for the next day. Washing their nets cleansed them from what they had experienced in the past and prepared them for what was to come in the future.

> *Too often we see the net washing times of life as licking our wounds from a prior defeat rather than preparation for the next harvest to come.*

Unfortunately, too often in our lives when we have an unsuccessful experience, we completely give up on what it is God has called us to do. Or, equally as devastating, too often we see the net washing times of life as licking our wounds from a prior defeat rather than preparation for the next harvest to come.

❧ Applying the Word ❧

How often do you hear the voice of God? What are some of the things He's said to you recently?

_____
_____
_____
_____
_____
_____
_____

Which of your everyday, ordinary activities do you need to surrender to Christ?

_____
_____
_____
_____
_____
_____
_____

What parts of your life have become brittle, rough and unusable? What do you think caused these areas of your life to become this way?

_____
_____
_____
_____
_____
_____

What net washing times in your life do you need to no longer view as times of defeat but rather as preparation for the next harvest?

_____
_____
_____
_____
_____
_____

As a result of the Word I just received, I know God wants me to…

_____
_____
_____
_____
_____
_____

LAUNCH OUT INTO THE DEEP

I'm going to start applying this to my life by…

_____
_____
_____
_____
_____
_____

But don't just listen to God's word. You must do what it says. Otherwise, you are only fooling yourselves.
James 1:22 NLT

Week 3

Let Jesus in Your Vessel

Let's take a look at Luke 5:3. It says:

> Then He got into one of the boats, which was Simon's, and asked him to put out a little from the land. And He sat down and taught the multitudes from the boat.

There is way more to this one verse than meets the eye. Let's take a few minutes to pick it apart. Once again, the *He* being referred to in this verse is Jesus. So, according to this verse, Jesus got into *one* of the boats. It did not say Jesus got into both of the boats. It says He got into one of the boats. This means Jesus had to make a choice. The good news that we can take away from this illustration is the fact that Jesus has options and He chooses you!

> *Jesus has options and He chooses you!*

Notice the profession of the man Jesus was addressing. He wasn't a doctor. He wasn't a high-powered attorney. He was a fisherman. God can use whatever sphere of influence you have and the experiences you've gained in whatever profession you're in to bring Himself glory! That's good news! So, whatever criteria you've used to disqualify yourself in the past, you now know it's invalid. God can use you no matter where you come from, no matter what your profession and no matter any other self-limiting factors you may have placed upon yourself in the past.

> *God can use whatever sphere of influence you have and the experiences you've gained in whatever profession you're in to bring Himself glory!*

The verse says Jesus got into one of the boats. Now, we've already determined these were no ordinary boats. These were vessels. So, let's read the verse as Jesus got into one of the vessels. Whose vessel did Jesus choose in this case? Simon's (also known as Peter).

I can't help but pause here a minute to point out just one chapter prior in Luke 4, it mentions Jesus had dinner at Simon Peter's house and healed his mother-in-law. Now, even though I believe chronologically Jesus' visit to Simon's house likely happened after Jesus' visit to Simon's boat, it does cause one to think. Too often we can know who Jesus is, what He can do and what He has done in the lives of others and yet we still do not fully trust Him with our lives or walk in the fullness of what it is He's asking us to do.

The verse then goes on to say that Jesus asked Simon. It doesn't say Jesus told Simon or Jesus forced Simon. It says Jesus asked

LET JESUS IN YOUR VESSEL

Simon. Why? Because Jesus will ask you if He can use your vessel. He will not force Himself on you. He wants you to be a willing vessel. What Jesus asked Simon to do was to put out a little from the land. Notice Jesus only asked Simon to put out a little. Too often we act as if Jesus is requiring so much of us and all He's asking for is a little. The Bible tells us in Luke 16:10 that he who is faithful with little will be faithful with much. God created us with a will of our own which means we have a right to choose. God doesn't force us to choose Him and His way, He wants us to choose Him and His way. So, Simon had to choose to submit to Jesus' request.

> *God created us with a will of our own which means we have a right to choose.*

If you know anything about Peter, you know he had a tendency to be all over the place. Let's just say his attention span seemed to be very short. But since he chose to put out a little from the land as Jesus asked of him, that would mean he would be a captive audience and would have a front row seat to whatever Jesus was ministering that day. No doubt, Jesus knows how to get our attention! And there's no doubt that Jesus knows what He's doing because we've already established that faith comes by hearing. So, if Peter had a front row seat and couldn't go anywhere, Jesus knew that Simon Peter's faith would be built that day.

The verse then goes on to say Jesus sat down. Wait a minute. Jesus sat down? Why would Jesus sit down? When I go to visit someone, I only sit down when I'm planning on sticking around for a while. I believe this was the case with Jesus. Jesus made Himself comfortable. He knew He was going to be there for a while. What's comical to me about this scene is it meant a very impatient Simon had no choice but to be patient. So, what did Jesus do when He sat down? He taught the multitudes from Simon's vessel.

❧ Applying the Word ❧

List some of the people in your sphere of influence. How have you influenced each of these people spiritually?

_____
_____
_____
_____
_____
_____

List some of the experiences you have gained to date. Which of these experiences have you consciously used to bring God glory?

_____
_____
_____
_____

What has been your relationship with Jesus up until this point? Do you fully trust Him with your life and walk in the fullness of what it is He is asking you to do?

_____
_____
_____
_____
_____
_____

What request has God made of you that you still have not submitted to? Why is this the case?

_____
_____
_____
_____
_____
_____

Have you been patient enough with God to allow Him to get comfortable in your vessel? Explain.

_____
_____
_____
_____
_____
_____

Are you willing to allow God to use your vessel to bring forth His Word? If so, how?

_____
_____
_____
_____
_____
_____

As a result of the Word I just received, I know God wants me to…

_____
_____
_____
_____
_____
_____

I'm going to start applying this to my life by…

_____
_____
_____
_____
_____
_____

But don't just listen to God's word. You must do what it says. Otherwise, you are only fooling yourselves.
James 1:22 NLT

Week 4

Here Are Your Instructions

Let's move on to Luke 5:4. It says:

> When He had stopped speaking, He said to Simon, "Launch out into the deep and let down your nets for a catch."

Notice this verse says, "When He had stopped speaking, He said to Simon." Don't you find it interesting that Jesus waited until He had finished speaking to the multitudes before He addressed Simon Peter? For me, this was a sweet reminder that we have to be patient and wait on God's timing. We can't force God to speak to us when we're ready to hear from Him. We just have to be attentive and wait on His timing. When Jesus did address Simon, He issued both a command and a promise. The command was for Simon to launch out into the deep. The promise was if Simon obeyed the command, he would receive a catch. Simon was guaranteed victory

> *We are guaranteed victory if we are willing to be obedient to the Father's instructions. Our Father delights in rewarding our obedience!*

even before he ever decided to obey Jesus' command. How much more true is that in the life of the believer today? We are guaranteed victory if we are willing to be obedient to the Father's instructions. Our Father delights in rewarding our obedience! He enjoys blessing us when we are a willing vessel and are obedient to Him. If we're going to be followers of Christ, we not only have to do what He says do, we have to do it when He says do it and how He says do it. We don't get to do what we want, when we want and how we want and still receive the same reward. Just like Simon had to do something to receive his natural reward, we have to do something to receive our eternal rewards.

Here's something I think is worth pointing out… Launching out into the deep for a catch was not the way fishermen of that day usually fished. They would tend to stay in the shallow end, let down their nets, then cinch them up and bring in the catch. This being the case, you'll notice Jesus' instructions to Simon were the exact opposite of what was usual and customary. Since Simon was a professional fisherman, his pride could have easily gotten in the way when this "carpenter" told him to do it differently than his own professional training and experience would have dictated.

Did you also notice that Jesus didn't give Simon new nets when He gave him his instructions? Simon simply had to use what he already had. Too often we convince ourselves that we can't do what God has asked us to do because we don't have what we need in order to do it. Or, if we do have it, we allow ourselves to make excuses such as it's too old, it's not good enough, it's not big enough or I tried using this the last time and it didn't work. But let's think about it this way. If God asked us to do something and He didn't provide us with anything new in which to do it, then automatically that should tell us that what we already have is

> *Whatever it is we have in our hands can be used by God to accomplish supernatural things!*

sufficient. Just like the words God spoke to Moses from the burning bush, we have to ask ourselves – What's that you have in your hands? Whatever it is we have in our hands can be used by God to accomplish supernatural things!

❧ Applying the Word ❧

In what area of your life is it that you just can't seem to wait on God's timing?

_____
_____
_____
_____
_____
_____

What is it that God has asked you to do and you still haven't done it yet?

___

What is it that you already have that you aren't allowing God to use?

___

In what way have you allowed pride to get in the way and potentially is preventing you from receiving the reward God has in store for you?

___

Here Are Your Instructions

As a result of the Word I just received, I know God wants me to...

_____
_____
_____
_____
_____
_____
_____

I'm going to start applying this to my life by...

_____
_____
_____
_____
_____
_____

But don't just listen to God's word. You must do what it says.
Otherwise, you are only fooling yourselves.
James 1:22 NLT

Week 5

This is Hard Work

> But Simon answered and said to Him, "Master, we have toiled all night and caught nothing; nevertheless at your word I will let down the net."
> (Luke 5:5)

The first word that stood out to me in this verse is the word *answered*. Usually we answer when someone has asked us a question. When it said Simon answered Jesus, the first thing I did was to go back to the previous verse looking for the question Jesus asked in the first place. It was then that I realized that Jesus didn't ask Simon Peter a question in the previous verse. He gave him an instruction. So why would Simon be answering if Jesus didn't ask him a question? How often do we do this in our lives? Way too often we respond to the King of Kings as if He asked us a question when in actuality He has issued us a command.

The next thing I noticed is that Simon Peter addressed Jesus as *Master*. This suggests to me that Simon Peter knew Jesus was a person of authority and so if nothing else, Simon Peter may have done what Jesus instructed out of respect and obedience and not necessarily out of love and faith. This is a direct reflection of Simon Peter's relationship with Jesus at this point. There has to come a point in our relationship with Christ where we're not just doing what He has asked of us out of obedience, but that we do what He asks of us out of our love for Him.

As if Jesus didn't already know, Simon Peter took the time to explain to Him that they had toiled all night and hadn't caught anything. They were extremely tired, but isn't that to be expected? We will always be extremely tired when we attempt to do things in our own strength. That's why we need the help of the Holy Spirit!

If we didn't already know it, Simon Peter's statement here informs us that fishing for fish is hard work. Well, if fishing for fish is hard work, what makes us think fishing for men would be any less work? Why is it that we're willing to work so hard for the things of this world all while thinking the things of God should come so easily?

> *Why is it that we're so willing to work so hard for temporary rewards and so unwilling to put in at least an equal amount of effort for eternal ones?*

In one breath we try to sound spiritual by saying we're "unworthy" while at the same time our actions scream "we are entitled." Why is it that we're so willing to work so hard for temporary rewards and so unwilling to put in at least an equal amount of effort for eternal ones?

Let me remind you again that we're talking about professional fishermen here. They were not amateurs, they were experts. So, if they hadn't caught anything already, there wasn't anything to catch. Besides, what does "a carpenter" know about fishing anyway?

Notice Simon Peter said they had toiled all night. Night time was the best time to catch fish. After the hot beaming sun had set, the fish were more likely to come closer to the surface of the water making it easier for them to be caught. So, if these professional fishermen had not caught anything all night, why would they catch anything now in the heat of the day?

The fact that they had not caught anything caused me to ask myself yet another question. (If you haven't already noticed, I do that a lot!) If they hadn't caught anything, why were they cleaning their nets three verses ago? Had their nets accumulated a bunch of useless stuff that needed to be cleaned out before the nets could serve their purpose? Even though we already previously established the need for washing the nets, I don't want to pass up the opportunity to point out that many times in our lives our reason for doing what we do is not always the same as the reason why it needs to be done. So, was it Simon Peter's pride that kept him looking busy but accomplishing nothing? Did he want to continue to look productive to lessen the blow to his ego of coming back to shore empty-handed? How often do we ourselves do this? How often do we continue in some vain activity even though it's producing no fruit? How often do we simply go through the motions in an attempt to make ourselves feel better or look better in the eyes of others? How often does our ego cause us to hold on to something longer or tighter than we should?

At some point during the previous night's fishing excursion, Simon Peter finally surrendered, accepted the fact they had caught nothing and went back to the shore to wash their nets. Even though Simon Peter felt the need to point this out, Jesus already knew they had worked all night, hadn't caught anything and were in need. And even though the content of the message that Jesus shared with the multitudes is not recorded in this passage of scripture, I'm sure Jesus shared something that might have caused Simon to think maybe Jesus could help them. If this were the case, why wouldn't he just ask Jesus for help? Well, just like it is for many of us, "I need help" is one of the three hardest things for us to say. What are the other two? "I love you" and "I'm sorry." At the source of this struggle is pride. Pride will often times lead to a lot of unmet needs and missed opportunities.

> *Pride will often times lead to a lot of unmet needs and missed opportunities.*

Let's look again at the first part of Simon Peter's statement to Jesus. He said, "We have toiled all night and caught nothing." I believe there are many lessons we can learn from this one statement. One of the major lessons I think we can learn is if we can be consistently successful on our own, there's no need for us to follow Christ. This is where I believe many of us go wrong today. We define our success according to the terms set by the world and when we reach a certain level of accomplishment we give ourselves all the praise, honor and glory. Who needs a heavenly Father when we continuously worship ourselves? For this very reason, I believe Simon Peter's statement can also encourage us not to get upset or discouraged over our failures. It is our failures that will make us more willing to follow Christ and less likely to worship ourselves.

> *It is our failures that will make us more willing to follow Christ and less likely to worship ourselves.*

Lastly, we can also learn from Simon Peter's statement that often times our greatest struggles will come in our area of greatest strength. God, in His infinite wisdom, will often times use our area of expertise to minister to us. Whenever we encounter someone who is better at something that we're good at, they somehow naturally have a tendency to capture our attention. What better way for Jesus to get Simon Peter's attention than through the very thing he was most passionate about?

After all of that, Simon Peter finally concedes and says, "nevertheless, at your word I will let down the net." Upon reading that, it made me wonder if this compliance was a reflection of Simon Peter's obedience and trust or was this simply his disclaimer. In other words, was Simon essentially saying to Jesus, "Now, I've already warned you. There's nothing out there. So don't blame me when we go through all of this and still come back empty-handed."

We can't be exactly sure of Simon Peter's thoughts or his motives in this instance, but we can attempt to place ourselves in his shoes. What thoughts do you think you would have in this situation? How do you think you would have responded? Remember… You're tired, probably hungry, and ready to go home. I don't think we have to attempt to envision ourselves on Simon Peter's fishing vessel to answer these questions. I'm sure we have at some point experienced a similar scenario in our own modern day lives. We just got off work, we just finished serving all day at church, we just finished babysitting that single mom's high energy children. How dare you now come and ask me to do something else? If those of us who have already accepted Christ have thoughts like these, we can only imagine what may have been running through Simon Peter's mind since he at this point had not yet decided to follow Christ. No matter what Simon Peter's thoughts and motives were, the bottom line is that he did what it was Jesus instructed him to do and there is

> *You won't always understand why God tells you to do something, but do it anyway!*

a valuable lesson we can all learn from this. You won't always understand why God tells you to do something, but do it anyway!

❧ Applying the Word ☙

What is it in your life that you have been toiling with all night long and have nothing to show for it?

_____
_____
_____
_____
_____

Is this something you've been toiling with and you shouldn't be or do you have nothing to show for it because the Master hasn't been in your vessel?

_____
_____
_____
_____
_____

Take a few minutes to examine your nets (heart & mind). What useless things have you accumulated in your nets that you need to have washed clean?

_____
_____
_____
_____
_____

Are there any pride issues in your life that keep you looking busy but accomplishing very little or nothing at all?

_____
_____
_____
_____
_____
_____

What is it that you're really good at that you need to release and allow God to show you that He's even better at it?

_____
_____
_____
_____
_____

This Is Hard Work

As a result of the Word I just received, I know God wants me to...

_____

_____

_____

_____

_____

I'm going to start applying this to my life by...

_____

_____

_____

_____

_____

_____

But don't just listen to God's word. You must do what it says.
Otherwise, you are only fooling yourselves.
James 1:22 NLT

Week 6

The Blessing of Help and Obedience

> And when they had done this, they caught a great number of fish, and their net was breaking.
> (Luke 5:6)

Notice the use of the word *they* in this passage. The "they" being referred to here is not Simon Peter and Jesus but rather Simon Peter and Andrew. Andrew, Simon Peter's brother, was on the boat with him. The two of them had just experienced the miraculous. They had received a harvest that no one could have brought in on their own. If Peter would have attempted to bring in such a harvest by himself, he would have lost more fish than he would have gained. Too often, we get selfish when God is moving in our lives. We get greedy, possessive and territorial. God is a God of more than enough. Whenever He blesses us, there's no need for us to try to hold on to all of it for ourselves. He blesses us so we can be a blessing to others. No matter what sibling rivalries Simon and Andrew may have had previously, I'm sure he was more than grateful that Andrew was there with him in the boat at that time.

God has an amazing way of placing the right people in our lives at exactly the right time with the right gifts and abilities to help us do what He's called us to do. We have to recognize and value the gift, and we have to learn to ask for and accept the help. Envision Peter trying to bring in this catch by himself. He would have exerted way more energy. He would have lost more fish than he would have gained. He would have been exhausted by the end of it. And he probably would have walked away more disappointed than grateful. The fact of the matter is that Peter needed Andrew. God has sent and placed people in your life for a reason. You need them. You need their help. You need their strength. You need their wisdom. You need their expertise. You need their encouragement. God has an amazing way of housing the very things we need inside other people.

The reverse is also true. Just like God sends people into your life for them to help you, He will send you into other people's lives for you to help them. We cannot accomplish any vision that God has given us on our own. We can bring in an even greater supernatural harvest when we ask for help. We can't bring in the harvest God has for us if we try to do it alone. If it is something we can accomplish on our own, then it's probably something we conjured up on our own.

> *We cannot accomplish any vision that God has given us on our own.*

THE BLESSING OF HELP AND OBEDIENCE

Let me take this opportunity to address another important issue that is going to be critical for us to understand as we launch out into the deep. God gives each of His children different gifts. There are some people who are gifted by God to help. They in no way should be forced, pressured into or made to feel guilty for not leading. At the same time, there are some people who are gifted by God to lead. They in no way should be forced or pressured into always remaining behind the scenes. If someone is gifted by God to help, then their assignment will involve helping. God will strategically place these amazingly gifted people on the "boat" of your life to help you, just like Andrew was on Peter's boat to help him. Had either one of them tried to take on the other person's role, the gospels would read much differently. We have to embrace the assignment God Has for us and the assignments He has for those around us. We don't need to apologize for it and we don't need to try to change it. Whatever assignment God has given each of us is significant in the Kingdom of God. When we get to heaven, we will be held accountable for what God assigned us to do not what man expected us to do.

> *Whatever assignment God has given each of us is significant in the Kingdom of God.*

The second half of this verse says their net was breaking. Why do you think their net was breaking? Do you think it was in poor condition? Do you think it was because of the number of fish they were trying to bring in with that one net? Why would Jesus send them out to do the impossible and not provide them with the tools they needed to accomplish it? Well, if we would just remind ourselves of the instructions that Jesus gave them two verses ago, we would notice Jesus specifically instructed them to let down their nets (plural) for a catch and yet they only let down their net (singular). Simon literally half did what Jesus instructed him to do. I'm sure in that moment he totally felt overwhelmed by something that was intended to be a blessing. Sometimes when the blessings of God are poured out on you, it may feel overwhelming if you haven't fully followed the instructions He gave you to prepare you to receive the blessing. Sadly enough, in situations like this, we often times will look at God as if it's His fault.

Why is it that we insist on blaming God for the outcome of certain things in our lives when it was we ourselves who chose not to follow the instructions He gave us? Did they only let down one net because they thought they knew best? Were they relying on their previous experience and thinking they wouldn't catch anything at all? Were they trying to avoid the additional work of washing two empty nets when they got back to shore? Whatever the case may be, their disobedience almost cost them their harvest. I can hear some of you saying to yourself, "Well, at least they let down one net. We should at least give them credit for that." While that may soothe

> *Partial obedience is disobedience.*

our conscience, we must acknowledge the fact that partial obedience is disobedience. Many times we as Christians only partially do what it is the Father instructs us to do and yet we expect to receive His full blessing. Jesus told them to let down their nets (plural) so they would be prepared to receive what He knew He had in store for them. Too often we want the abundant blessings of God but we don't want to go through the process of preparation that is necessary for us to be ready to receive it.

☙ Applying the Word ❧

What amazing things has God done in your life recently?

_____
_____
_____
_____
_____
_____

What spiritual gift(s) has God given you? Are you operating in your gift or attempting to operate in someone else's?

_____
_____
_____
_____
_____
_____

Who are the people that God has placed you in their life for you to help them? Have you helped them in the way God has instructed you?

_____
_____
_____
_____
_____

How many "fish" would you say you've lost in your life because you didn't accept the help God sent you to help bring in the catch? Explain.

_____
_____
_____
_____
_____

In what areas of your life has God told you to let down your nets (plural) and you've only let down your net (singular)? Why were you disobedient in this way?

_____
_____
_____
_____
_____

The Blessing Of Help And Obedience

As a result of the Word I just received, I know God wants me to…

_____
_____
_____
_____
_____
_____

I'm going to start applying this to my life by…

_____
_____
_____
_____
_____
_____

But don't just listen to God's word. You must do what it says.
Otherwise, you are only fooling yourselves.
James 1:22 NLT

Week 7

The Beauty of Repentance and Humility

> So they signaled to their partners in the other boat to come and help them. And they came and filled both the boats, so that they began to sink. When Simon Peter saw it, he fell down at Jesus' knees, saying, "Depart from me, for I am a sinful man, O Lord!" For he and all who were with him were astonished at the catch of fish which they had taken.
> (Luke 5:7–9)

> *Just when we humble ourselves enough to ask for help, we probably will have to humble ourselves again to ask for even more.*

The "partners" this verse refers to are James and John. It says they asked them to come and help them. Peter had already gained the assistance of Andrew and yet the two of them still needed to ask for more help. What a great reminder for us in our lives. We will always need more help than we think we do. Just when we humble ourselves enough to ask for help, we probably will have to humble ourselves again to ask for even more. The very next words in this verse say, "and they came." The beautiful thing about us living our lives with Jesus in our boat is that He will always provide willing and skilled laborers to help us accomplish what it is He has for us to do. These men brought in so many fish that their boats began to sink. With this kind of harvest, Simon Peter not only needed people to help him bring it in, he also needed people to share it with.

Simon Peter had just witnessed a miracle and suddenly he was humbled to the point of repentance. As servants of Jesus Christ, we have to learn to be humble. Without humility, pride will lead us to believe the miracles that God works in our lives were simply things we did on our own as a result of our own intelligence. We must be purposeful about giving God His glory.

> *We have to consciously keep God in the forefront or we will sometimes subconsciously leave Him in the background.*

We have to consciously keep God in the forefront or we will sometimes subconsciously leave Him in the background. Peter admits to Jesus that he is a sinful man. Exactly what sin was Peter referring to? Maybe it was pride or maybe it was fear. Maybe it was doubt or lack of faith. Maybe it was resentment or possibly even offense. Whatever the case may be, he saw the need to repent and he did.

The Beauty Of Repentance And Humility

This time when Simon Peter addressed Jesus, he didn't address him as Master as he had done three verses ago. Rather, this time he refers to Him as Lord. Isn't it amazing how our relationship with God so drastically changes when we have an encounter with Him and experience Him for ourselves?

Verse nine says not only was Simon Peter astonished, but also all who were with him. Peter, just like you and I, had a sphere of influence. Peter had influence with every person that helped him. Because he was willing to ask for help, others got the benefit of witnessing a miracle. When we open up our lives and share it with others, they not only reap the benefit of our blessings, they also get to experience the goodness of our God! God wants to move in our lives and He wants people to see it. I believe God sometimes does things in our lives so extravagantly to astonish us enough to know beyond a shadow of a doubt it wasn't anything we did in our own strength. What had just happened with these fishermen, they knew they did not do it themselves. They had already tried everything they knew to do and were unsuccessful. If they had only brought in a few fish they could have written it off as a coincidence. However, since they brought in more fish than they had ever brought in

> *When we open up our lives and share it with others, they not only reap the benefit of our blessings, they also get to experience the goodness of our God!*

before (even on their best day), they knew it had to be God and they couldn't take any of the credit for themselves.

❧ Applying the Word ☙

In what way has God been good to you and you still have not shared it with anyone else?

_____
_____
_____
_____
_____
_____

Who are the people you have in your life that are willing and able to help you and support you while you're out in the deep? Have you asked for and accepted their help or are you trying to navigate the deep all on your own?

_____
_____
_____
_____
_____
_____

The Beauty Of Repentance And Humility

What do you need to repent of right now?

_____
_____
_____
_____
_____
_____

In what areas of your life do you need to be more humble?

_____
_____
_____
_____
_____
_____

What are some things God has done in your life for which you have taken the credit for yourself?

_____
_____
_____
_____
_____
_____

As a result of the Word I just received, I know God wants me to…

_____
_____
_____
_____
_____
_____

I'm going to start applying this to my life by…

_____
_____
_____
_____
_____
_____

But don't just listen to God's word. You must do what it says.
Otherwise, you are only fooling yourselves.
James 1:22 NLT

Week 8

Fishermen will be Fishermen

---

and so also were James and John, the sons of Zebedee, who were partners with Simon. And Jesus said to Simon, "Do not be afraid. From now on you will catch men."
(Luke 5:10)

Midway through verse ten, Jesus addresses Simon. There were several men surrounding Jesus at this point. Why do you think Jesus chose to specifically address Simon Peter? Could it be because Simon Peter was the one who allowed Jesus to come into His vessel? Was Jesus already identifying Peter as a leader amongst this group? Could it have been the fact that Jesus knew that if he could make an impact in Simon Peter's life, that Simon would influence the lives of the other men? Was Jesus even at this point displaying the concept of multiplication long before the five loaves and two fish? I believe Jesus was demonstrating a valuable principle that we all need to understand – that if we desire to add growth we need to lead followers but if we desire to multiply growth we need to lead leaders. Jesus knew that by impacting the life of the leader He would impact the lives of everyone who followed him.

LAUNCH OUT INTO THE DEEP

The first thing Jesus told Simon Peter was, "Do not be afraid." What do you think Peter may have been afraid of? Afraid of God's presence? Afraid of God's power? Afraid to leave his job? Afraid to start something new? Afraid of what people may think? Afraid of the work that God was about to call him to do? Afraid of someone as common as him being connected with someone as powerful as Jesus? Or do you think maybe he was simply afraid to trust Jesus?

As odd as it may sound, many times we are more comfortable trusting in ourselves than in the One who created us. It is very possible that Simon Peter and his team of fishermen may have found more safety, security and significance in their fishing then they did in the One who just helped them to bring in the biggest catch of their lives. Fishing, they knew. Jesus, they just met. Even though He had done more for them in one day than they possibly had done for themselves over an extended period of time, natural human tendency is to be afraid of what is unknown and what we don't understand. We are more comfortable trusting the little that we know than taking a risk to possibly learn something greater. Anything we trust in more than we trust in God is an idol. Even our job can be an idol in our lives. Up until this point, these men were defined by their fishing. But in an instant, Jesus revealed Himself to these

> *We are more comfortable trusting the little that we know than taking a risk to possibly learn something greater.*

men as Jehovah Jireh. Their provision no longer needed to come from fishing but now could come from the One who commands the fish and they obey.

Jesus goes on to tell Peter, "From now on you will catch men." How do you think you would have responded if someone told you this? This was definitely not a comment they would have ever heard before and certainly not something they had ever done before. Yet, knowing all of this, Jesus still made the declaration over them.

So many of us convince ourselves we are of no benefit to the Kingdom. We tell ourselves we're not smart enough or not experienced enough. We think we're not gifted enough or we don't know enough of the Word. Whatever our excuse may have been up until this point, we must let it go if we want to launch out into the deep. We have to know for ourselves that God can take whatever it is we're doing right now and use it for His glory. So, we need to stop complaining and get the training. I don't know if you noticed it or not, but Jesus didn't change what these men were doing. He simply changed the harvest it produced. Simon Peter went from fishing for fish to sustain natural life to fishing for men to obtain eternal life.

ॐ Applying the Word ॐ

Are you afraid of trusting Jesus? If so, why? If not, how did you come to this level of trust?

_____
_____
_____
_____
_____
_____

What is it you're afraid of that's preventing you from launching out into the deep?

_____
_____
_____
_____
_____
_____

What is it you're trusting in so much that it's giving you an artificial sense of safety, security, and significance and possibly becoming a false idol in your life?

_____
_____
_____
_____
_____
_____

FISHERMEN WILL BE FISHERMEN

What is it that you're already doing that God wants to use for the kingdom? What adjustments need to be made in what you're doing to move it from a natural perspective to a Kingdom perspective?

_____
_____
_____
_____
_____
_____

As a result of the Word I just received, I know God wants me to…

_____
_____
_____
_____
_____
_____

I'm going to start applying this to my life by…

_____
_____
_____
_____
_____
_____

But don't just listen to God's word. You must do what it says. Otherwise, you are only fooling yourselves.
James 1:22 NLT

Week 9

This Way to the Deep

> So when they had brought their boats to land, they forsook all and followed Him.
> (Luke 5:11)

Since the men are just now bringing their boats back to land, that means all the miraculous things that happened before now all happened on the boat in the deep. Right? That means Jesus didn't send Simon Peter out into the deep alone. He went with him. So often we fear stepping out into the unknown. When this fear tries to grip us, all we have to do is trust the fact that if God sent us, He will be with us.

There are certain miracles we simply will not experience if we choose to continue to wade in the shallow end of life. I believe there are certain miracles that are reserved for the deep places. My family and I went on a cruise a few years ago. It baffles my mind to this day to

> *There are certain miracles we simply will not experience if we choose to continue to wade in the shallow end of life.*

think that the ship we were on was five times bigger than the Titanic at 1,187 feet long and 240 feet high, carrying over 8,000 people on board its 16 decks weighing in at about 100,000 tons. In some respects, I'd say it's just shy of a miracle that something that massive can float! Now try to imagine this same ship in your local community swimming pool. Impossible! There is a whole new realm of possibility in the deep that is simply not available to us in the shallow. Once you've gotten a taste of what's available to you in the deep, the shallow simply no longer satisfies.

After these men had their experience with Jesus in the deep, they chose to leave everything behind and followed Him. Going back to business as usual was no longer an option for them after what they had just experienced. Even their best fishing day would have been disappointing now that their realm of possibility had just been significantly broadened. What an amazing testimony all of us could have. Just like Simon Peter, our obedience to the Father could result in the people in our sphere of influence also choosing to follow Christ and life as they once knew it would no longer be the same. You don't have to have a gift of evangelism to win people to Christ. You can win people to Christ or turn them away from Christ simply based on your behavior and the choices you

> *You don't have to have a gift of evangelism to win people to Christ. You can win people to Christ or turn them away from Christ simply based on your behavior and the choices you make.*

make. Just like that, these men went from being dedicated to their profession to being dedicated to God.

In order for us to completely follow Christ, there are some things in our lives that we are going to have to leave behind. In Simon Peter's case, there was no possible way he could have effectively followed Jesus if he tried to hang on to his boat. For many of us, what we will have to leave behind may be our comfort zones or the things we find familiar. The place we currently live, the friends we currently have, our current daily routine. What's interesting to me is that many of the familiar things in our lives that we try so desperately to hold on to are often times things we no longer even desire. We would rather hold on to an undesired familiar than to follow Jesus into the unknown. Why are we so unwilling to exchange the stagnant, fruitless routine of our daily lives for the exciting adventure of following the leading of the Holy Spirit? Is it the fear of the unknown? Is it the lack of control? Is it misplaced priorities? Is it simply a reflection of a life lived solely for the here and now rather than for eternity? Often times we will be required to make a choice. Either Jesus will be Lord of all or He won't be Lord at all.

We can believe in Christ and live a boring life but it is impossible to live a boring life if we're actually following Him! Are you living a boring life? Is it possible that maybe you believe in Christ but you're not following Him? Could it be that Jesus is your savior but you haven't yet made Him your Lord? If that is the case for you, I challenge you today to make Jesus the Lord of your life. Relinquish control of your life to Him. Commit to being obedient to Him and follow wherever He leads you. Your life will never be the same!

❧ Applying the Word ❧

What cruise ships are you trying to get to float in your community swimming pool?

_____
_____
_____
_____
_____

Is your behavior and the choices you're making winning people to Christ or turning them away from Christ? Give some examples.

_____
_____
_____
_____
_____

What are things in your life that you need to forsake / let go / leave behind in order to follow Jesus?

_____
_____
_____
_____
_____
_____

Are you following Jesus because of who He is or because of what He can do?

_____
_____
_____
_____
_____

As a result of the Word I just received, I know God wants me to…

_____
_____
_____
_____
_____
_____

LAUNCH OUT INTO THE DEEP

I'm going to start applying this to my life by...

_____
_____
_____
_____
_____
_____

But don't just listen to God's word. You must do what it says.
Otherwise, you are only fooling yourselves.
James 1:22 NLT

Week 10

Exactly What is Deep

With God, all things are possible. If Jesus can get a fisherman hooked, then He can get a doctor or a nurse healed! He can get a lawyer convicted (by the Holy Spirit)! He can cause a mother to give birth to her dreams! He can get a secretary to take note! He can get a cook to feed on the Word of God! He can get a banker to invest in the Kingdom! He can get a teacher to learn His Word! He can get a speech pathologist to speak boldly! And He can get you to navigate the deep if you're willing to launch out!

So, exactly what is deep? Deep is going to mean different things to different people. What is deep for one may be shallow for another. My children are excellent swimmers. They are drawn to the water. Whenever they go to a swimming pool, they immediately head for the deep end and they jump right in – no life jacket or anything. Twelve feet is a minimum for them. That's where their fun begins. The tall twisting slides, the incredibly high diving boards – they'll spend hours going on them over and over again. Not I, on the other hand. If you

> *What is deep for one may be shallow for another.*

can get me to a swimming pool, five feet is about my max. I simply don't want the water to be deeper than I can stand in. What is deep and scary to me is fun and exciting to them. This is much like it is in our spiritual lives. What is fun and exciting to one may be way too deep for another. I think sometimes as Christians, in our zeal, we inadvertently drive people farther away from Christ by prematurely trying to get them to wade in the spiritual twelve feet deep waters when five feet is plenty deep for where they currently are in their walk with Christ.

Here's something that's very important for all of us to remember…Please don't ever compare your deep to someone else's deep because inevitably, you'll walk away thinking one of your deeps is shallow. We don't have to overcomplicate this. Jesus made this very simple. He took a group of fishermen deep sea fishing. Sometimes God just wants us to go deeper in what we've already been doing. Maybe today God just wants you to go deeper in your level of commitment and involvement with Him. Maybe He wants you to start that new business. Maybe He wants you to accept that promotion. Maybe He wants you to go on that mission's trip. Maybe He wants you to quit that job. Maybe He wants you to go back to school. Maybe He wants you to give more offering. Maybe He wants you to move to another state. Maybe He wants you to get married. Maybe He wants you to be a stay-at-home mom. Maybe He wants you to go to counseling. Maybe He wants you to ask for help. Maybe He wants you to retire from the world so you can serve full time for the Kingdom. Maybe He wants you to follow after that dream everyone has been telling you is unattainable. The possibilities are endless. The only way you'll know is to have the conversation with Him.

Yes, I know. It can be scary out in the deep. You may not want to go. Maybe you've never been there before. Maybe you're paralyzed by the unknown. If you're like me, your first thought may have been, "But they're sharks out there in the deep!" Or, maybe your thoughts lean towards the fact that you don't know how to swim or you've never been in water past your knees or you feel like you might drown out there. Well, when you feel like you're drowning in the sea of life, you don't have to worry. All you have to do is remember your Lifeguard walks on water!

> *When you feel like you're drowning in the sea of life, you don't have to worry. All you have to do is remember your Lifeguard walks on water!*

My oldest son is a lifeguard. One of the things they teach them when they go through their certification training is if a person is fighting the water or if they're fighting the lifeguard, they are to wait until the person gets tired of trying to save themselves and surrender before the lifeguard moves in to save them. This is a very natural principle that I believe God uses in the spiritual. Often times when we are screaming, desperate for God to save us, He is simply waiting for us to surrender. What is tiring and difficult for us to do in our strength is simple for God to do in His strength.

You have to use wisdom when you launch out into the deep. It is imperative that you don't go out there alone. You have to be sure God is with you. The deep is not the place to be playing around. You have to know there's a difference between getting yourself into deep water and launching out into the deep. If God didn't send you, don't you dare go. If He did send you, don't you dare stay. No matter how scary it may be, if He sent you, you can rest assured that He will be with you and He will protect you.

When you're just going to play around in the water, you wear a swimsuit. But, when you're launching out into the deep, you better have on your full armor! Every piece of that armor will be detrimental to your survival. Ephesians 6:10–18 says,

> Finally, my brethren, be strong in the Lord and in the power of his might. Put on the whole armor of God, that you may be able to stand against the wiles of the devil. For we do not wrestle against flesh and blood, but against principalities, against powers, against the rulers of the darkness of this age, against spiritual hosts of wickedness in the heavenly places. Therefore take up the whole armor of God, that you may be able to withstand in the evil day, and having done all, stand. Stand

therefore having girded your waist with truth, having put on the breastplate of righteousness, and having shod your feet with the preparation of the gospel of peace; above all, taking the shield of faith with which you will be able to quench all the fiery darts of the wicked one. And take the helmet of salvation, and the sword of the Spirit, which is the word of God; praying always with all prayer and supplication in the Spirit, being watchful to this and with all perseverance and supplication for all the saints.

Now here's the beauty of the entire experience… Once you've launched out into the deep with Jesus in your vessel, it makes it just that much easier to do it again. It makes it that much easier to go even deeper the next time. As we just learned, the first time Jesus asked Simon Peter to launch out into the deep and let down his nets for a catch in Luke 5, he wasn't too sure about it. But the next time he received these instructions from Jesus in John 21, he didn't even hesitate. He had learned from experience, from a previous encounter with Jesus, the blessing he would receive if he would just do what He said!

Applying the Word

What is your deep?

_____
_____
_____
_____
_____

What is there about the deep that makes you afraid?

_____
_____
_____
_____
_____

Have you fully surrendered your life to Christ or are you still in some respects trying to save yourself?

_____
_____
_____
_____
_____
_____

Have you ever attempted to launch out into the deep on your own? If so, what was the outcome?

_____
_____
_____
_____
_____
_____

Which piece of the armor of God have you most frequently gone without? What will you begin to do to ensure you are fully dressed?

_____
_____
_____
_____
_____

As a result of the Word I just received, I know God wants me to…

_____
_____
_____
_____
_____
_____

LAUNCH OUT INTO THE DEEP

I'm going to start applying this to my life by…

_____
_____
_____
_____
_____
_____

But don't just listen to God's word. You must do what it says.
Otherwise, you are only fooling yourselves.
James 1:22 NLT

Week 11

Preparing for the Deep

We have covered so much in the last few weeks. If you have actually taken this study seriously, I know the Holy Spirit has spoken some things to your heart. Just when those things are ready to settle into your heart, the enemy will try to come and steal them away from you or try to convince you of something different. To help prevent this from happening, I want to slow us down just a little bit to reinforce some of the things we have already discussed. I want to remind you of some of the nuggets that the enemy may have tried to prevent you from getting. I want to help you to solidify that which the Holy Spirit has spoken to you in your heart.

Please don't rush through these. Take your time and meditate on them. Sincerely pray the prayer at the end of each section to ask God to help you. Remember, with God all things are possible!

- God can use the sphere of influence that you have and the experiences that you've gained in whatever profession you're in to bring Himself glory.

- We, just like nets, can become brittle, rough, and unusable if we're not washed (in the Word) frequently.

- Jesus has options and He chooses you!

PRAYER: God, please help me to accept the fact that You have chosen me.

- Jesus will ask you if He can use your vessel. He will never force Himself on you.

- If we're going to be followers of Christ, we not only have to do what He says to do, we have to do it when He says do it, and we have to do it how He says to do it.

- Jesus enjoys blessing us when we're willing to be used by Him and be obedient to Him.

- If you can be consistently successful on your own, then there's no need for you to follow Christ.

- Don't get upset or discouraged over your failures. It is your failures that will make you more willing to follow Christ.

- You won't always understand why God tells you to do something, but do it anyway.

PRAYER: God, please help me to be obedient even if I don't understand your plan.

- Just like God sends people into your life for them to help you, He will send you into other people's lives for you to help them.

- We cannot accomplish any vision that God has given us on our own.

- We have to embrace the assignment God Has for us and the assignments He has for those around us. We don't need to apologize for it and we don't need to try to change it.

- Whatever assignment God has given each of us is significant in the Kingdom of God.

PRAYER: God, please help me to accept and value the help you send me and help me to serve those I am sent to as serving unto the Lord.

- Partial obedience is disobedience.

- Sometimes you won't receive the blessing God has for you until you do what He tells you to do.

- Sometimes when the blessings of God are poured out on you, it may feel overwhelming if you haven't fully followed the instructions He gave you to prepare you to receive the blessing.

- God wants to bless you with a blessing so big, you're going to need people to help you and people to share it with.

- Without humility, pride will lead us to believe the miracles that God works in our lives were simply things we did on our own as a result of our own intelligence.

- We have to consciously keep God in the forefront or we will sometimes subconsciously leave Him in the background.

- If we desire to add growth we need to lead followers but if we desire to multiply growth we need to lead leaders.

- We are led by that in which we trust.

- Anything we trust in more than we trust in God is an idol.

- God can take whatever it is we're doing right now and use it for His glory. So, we need to stop complaining and get the training.

PRAYER: Father, please help me to stop murmuring and complaining and to be fully obedient to Your instructions.

- You don't have to have a gift of evangelism to win people to Christ. You can win people to Christ or turn them away from Christ simply based on your behavior and the choices you make.

- In order for us to completely follow Christ, there are some things in our lives that we're going to have to leave behind.

PRAYER: Father, please show me what I have to leave behind to fully follow you and then help me to trust You enough to do it.

- When launching out into the deep, please don't ever compare your deep to someone else's deep because inevitably, you'll walk away thinking one of your deeps is shallow.

- Sometimes God just wants us to go deeper in what we've already been doing.

- It can be scary out in the deep.

- When you feel like you're drowning in the sea of life, you don't have to worry. All you have to do is remember your Lifeguard walks on water!

- Once you've launched out into the deep with Jesus in your vessel, it makes it just that much easier to do it again.

PRAYER: Father, please help me not to fear the unknown.

- Don't launch out into the deep alone. Be sure God is with you.

- When you're just going to play around in the water, you wear a swimsuit. But, when you're launching out into the deep, you better have on your full armor (breastplate of righteousness, belt of truth, feet shod with the gospel of peace, shield of faith, helmet of salvation and the sword of the Spirit/Word)

- You have to know there's a big difference between getting yourself into deep water and launching out into the deep.

PRAYER: Father, please help me to be dressed in my full armor at all times and prepared for whatever comes my way.

Applying the Word

As a result of the Word I just received, I know God wants me to…

_____
_____
_____
_____
_____
_____

I'm going to start applying this to my life by…

_____
_____
_____
_____
_____
_____

But don't just listen to God's word. You must do what it says. Otherwise, you are only fooling yourselves.
James 1:22 NLT

Week 12

Launching Out Into the Deep!

We began this study by developing our definition of the term *launch out into the deep*.

Launch Out Into the Deep:
To propel yourself in a direction away from among others toward a position of contact that is definite or has been previously specified but that you may find difficult to penetrate or comprehend.

Just from this definition alone, I believe there are three very important things we can take away from it:

1. To propel yourself in a direction away from among others – It is time for you to come out from amongst the multitudes and become a true disciple of Christ.

2. Toward a position of contact that is definite or has been previously specified – You need to make the time to get

alone with God so you can hear His direction and plan for your life.

3. But that you may find difficult to penetrate or comprehend – You need to decide today to be committed to doing what God tells you to do even if you don't understand why.

I don't think it's a coincidence that Peter, James and John, three of the ones that launched out into the deep with Jesus, were also the ones who were a part of Jesus' inner circle and got to experience things with Jesus that the others didn't get to experience. In Mark 5, Peter, James and John were the only disciples with Jesus when He went to Jairus' house and raised his daughter from the dead. In Mark 14, Peter, James and John were the only disciples Jesus took with Him while He prayed in the garden of Gethsemane. In Matthew 17, Peter, James and John were the only disciples Jesus took with Him up the mountain to witness His transfiguration. In Luke 22, Peter and John were the only disciples Jesus sent to make preparations for the Passover. In John 19, John was the only disciple to witness Jesus' crucifixion and he was the one to whom Jesus left His mother's care after His death.

In passages throughout the scriptures, Peter's name is always listed first when he is included amongst the disciples in any given account. As documented in Matthew 14, Peter was the only disciple to ever walk on water with Jesus. It was to Peter that Jesus said in Matthew 16 "…upon this rock I will build my church." In

Matthew 17, Peter was the only disciple that Jesus sent to catch a fish with money in its mouth to pay their taxes. Peter was the first disciple to address the crowd in Jerusalem after the Holy Spirit came on the day of Pentecost in Acts 2. Peter was the first disciple to share the gospel with Gentiles and to witness the gift of the Holy Spirit being poured out on them. Before Jesus ascended into heaven, it was Peter to whom He specifically told to feed His sheep. Had we been talking about one or two occasions, we may have been able to write this off as a coincidence but I think with all the instances what were mentioned, there must be something to it. There must be more that we get to experience with God when we launch out into the deep.

So, if you want to go places that other disciples don't get to go, you better launch out into the deep. If you want to see things that other disciples don't get to see, you better launch out into the deep. If you want to do things that other disciples don't get to do, then you better stop playing around in the kiddie pool and launch out into the deep!

LAUNCH OUT INTO THE DEEP

❧ Applying the Word ❧

What is the "deep" that God wants you to launch out into?

_____
_____
_____
_____
_____

As a result of the Word I just received, I know God wants me to…

_____
_____
_____
_____
_____

I'm going to start applying this to my life by…

_____
_____
_____
_____
_____

But don't just listen to God's word. You must do what it says.
Otherwise, you are only fooling yourselves.
James 1:22 NLT

www.ingramcontent.com/pod-product-compliance
Ingram Content Group UK Ltd.
Pitfield, Milton Keynes, MK11 3LW, UK
UKHW022216230426
12048UKWH00016BA/874